THE NOBEL PEACE PRIZE
AND THE DALAI LAMA

THE NOBEL PEACE PRIZE AND THE DALAI LAMA

Foreword by Tenzin Tethong

Compiled and edited by Sidney Piburn

Snow Lion Publications
Ithaca, New York USA

Snow Lion Publications
P.O. Box 6483
Ithaca, NY 14851
USA

Copyright © 1990 His Holiness the Dalai Lama and Sidney Piburn

All rights reserved. No part of this book may be reproduced by any means without prior written permission from the publisher.

Printed in the USA

ISBN 0-937938-86-6

Library of Congress Cataloging-in-Publication Data

Bstan-'dzin-rgya-mtsho, Dalai Lama XIV, 1935-
  The Nobel Peace Prize and Dalai Lama / compiled and edited by
Sidney Piburn.
    p. cm.
  Includes biographical references.
  Contents: Announcement of the Nobel Peace Prize — Initial remarks
/ by the Dalai Lama — Statement of the Norwegian Nobel Committee —
Acceptance speech / by the Dalai Lama — Statement on use of the
prize monjey — Introductory remarks to the Nobel lecture — The
Nobel Peace Prize lecture / by the Dalai Lama — The Nobel evening
address / by the Dalai Lama — Concluding remarks / by the Nobel
Committee — Facts about Tibet.
  ISBN 0-937938-86-6
  1. Peace—Awards. 2. Nobel prizes. 3. Bstan-'dzin-rgya-mtsho,
Dalai Lama XIV, 1935-   I. Piburn, Sidney. II. Title.
JX1963.B7615 1990
327.1'72'092—dc20
                                                        90-31262
                                                            CIP

Table of Contents

Foreword

The presentation of the Nobel Prize to His Holiness the Fourteenth Dalai Lama stands as a testimony to the profound and far-reaching vision of His Holiness and the faith and determination of the Tibetan people. This book will become an important historical document for the Tibetan people and nation; therefore I am honored to write a few words of introduction.

The Nobel Committee must be applauded for presenting this prestigious award to His Holiness. The Nobel Peace Prize represents substantial international recognition of the long-suffering Tibetan people and their struggle for freedom under the leadership of a unique individual. By their recognition the Nobel Committee has advanced the work of peace initiated by His Holiness, and has thereby moved the world one step closer to making that peace a reality.

It was a great honor and privilege to be present in Aula Hall, Oslo, on December 10, 1989, when His Holiness received the award in a simple and dignified ceremony. Those few days in Oslo, shared with so many friends of Tibet, constituted such a historical and magical occasion that they could only be repeated in Lhasa.

Peace for Tibet and the world!

Tenzin N. Tethong
Special Representative of
HIS HOLINESS THE DALAI LAMA
Washington, D.C.
February 21, 1990

October 5

ANNOUNCEMENT

Announcement of the Award of the 1989 Nobel Peace Prize

The Norwegian Nobel Committee has decided to award the 1989 Nobel Peace Prize to the Fourteenth Dalai Lama, Tenzin Gyatso, the religious and political leader of the Tibetan people. The Committee wants to emphasize the fact that the Dalai Lama in his struggle for the liberation of Tibet consistently has opposed the use of violence. He has instead advocated peaceful solutions based upon tolerance and mutual respect in order to preserve the historical and cultural heritage of his people.

The Dalai Lama has developed his philosophy of peace from a great reverence for all things living and upon the concept of universal responsibility embracing all mankind as well as nature.

In the opinion of the Committee the Dalai Lama has come forward with constructive and forward-looking proposals for the solution of international conflicts, human rights issues, and global environmental problems.

Initial Remarks by His Holiness The Fourteenth Dalai Lama of Tibet On Being Awarded The Nobel Peace Prize
Oct. 5, 1989

I am deeply touched to be chosen as this year's recipient of the Nobel Peace Prize. I believe my selection reaffirms the universal values of non-violence, peace and understanding between all members of our great human family. We all desire a happier, more humane and harmonious world, and I have always felt that the practice of love and compassion, tolerance and respect for others is the most effective manner in which to bring this about.

I hope this prize will provide courage to the six million people of Tibet. For some forty years now, Tibetans have been undergoing the most painful period in our long history. During this time, over a million of our people perished and more than six thousand monasteries—the seat of our peaceful culture—were destroyed. There is not a single family, either in Tibet or among the refugees abroad, which has gone unscathed. Yet, our people's determination and commitment to spiritual values and the practice of non-violence remain unshaken. This prize is a profound recognition of their faith and perseverance.

The demonstrations which have rocked Tibet for the past two years continue to be non-violent despite brutal suppression. Since the imposition of martial law in Lhasa last March, Tibet has been sealed off, and while global attention has focused on the tragic events in China, a systematic effort to crush the spirit and national identity of the Tibetan people is being pursued by the government of the People's Republic.

Tibetans today are facing the real possibility of elimination as a people and a nation. The government of the People's Republic of China is practicing a form of genocide by relocating millions of Chinese settlers into Tibet. I ask that this massive population transfer be stopped. Unless the cruel and inhuman treatment of my people is brought to an end, and until they are given their due right to self-determination, there will always be obstacles in finding a solution to the Tibetan issue.

I accept the Nobel Peace Prize in a spirit of optimism despite the many grave problems which humanity faces today. We all know the immensity of the challenges facing our generation: the problem of overpopulation, the threat to our environment and the dangers of military confrontation. As this dramatic century draws to a close, it is clear that the renewed yearning for freedom and democracy sweeping the globe provides an unprecedented opportunity for building a better world. Freedom is the real source of human happiness and creativity. Only when it is allowed to flourish can a genuinely stable international climate exist.

The suppression of the rights and freedoms of any people by totalitarian governments is against human nature and the recent movements for democracy in various parts of the world is a clear indication of this.

The Chinese students have given me great hope for the future of China and Tibet. I feel that their movement follows in the tradition of Mahatma Gandhi's ahimsa or non-violence which has deeply inspired me ever since I was a small boy. The eventual success of all people seeking a more tolerant atmosphere must derive from a commitment to counter hatred and violence with patience. We must seek change through dialogue and trust.

It is my heartfelt prayer that Tibet's plight may be resolved in such a manner and that once again my country, the Roof of the World, may serve as a sanctuary of peace and a resource of spiritual inspiration at the heart of Asia.

I hope and pray that the decision to give me the Nobel Peace Prize will encourage all those who pursue the path of peace to do so in a renewed spirit of optimism and strength.

December 10

AWARD

Crowd outside His Holiness' hotel.   *Photo: Dr. Jan Andersson*

Statement of the Norwegian Nobel Committee
The 1989 Nobel Peace Prize

The Nobel Peace Prize is one of six awards bearing the name of Alfred Nobel that are presented today. Five of these awards are made in Stockholm, and the Norwegian Nobel Committee would like to take this opportunity to congratulate the laureates who will be honored in the Swedish capital today. This year's ceremony is an occasion of special gratification to us Norwegians, as one of the recipients is a Norwegian, Professor Trygve Haavelmo, the winner of this year's Nobel Prize for Economics. We would like to congratuate him on this honor.

This year's Nobel Peace Prize has been awarded to H.H. the Dalai Lama, first and foremost for his consistent resistance to the use of violence in his people's struggle to regain their liberty.

Ever since 1959, the Dalai Lama, together with some one hundred thousand of his countrymen, has lived in an organized community in exile in India. This is by no means the first community of exiles in the world, but it is assuredly the first and only one that has not set up any militant liberation movement.

This policy of non-violence is all the more remarkable when it is considered in relation to the sufferings inflicted on the Tibetan people during the occupation of their country. The Dalai Lama's response has been to propose a peaceful solution which would go a long way to satisfying Chinese interests. It would be difficult to cite any historical example of a minority's struggle to secure its rights, in which a more conciliatory attitude to the adversary has been adopted than in the case of the Dalai Lama. It would be natural to compare him with Mahatma Gandhi, one of this century's greatest protagonists of peace, and the Dalai Lama likes to consider himself one of Gandhi's successors. People have occasionally wondered why Gandhi himself was never awarded the Nobel Peace Prize, and the present Nobel Committee can with impunity share this surprise, while regarding this year's award of the prize as in part a tribute to the memory of Mahatma Gandhi. This year's laureate will also be able to celebrate a significant jubilee, as it is now fifty years since he was solemnly installed as H. H. the Fourteenth Dalai Lama of the Tibetan people, when he was four years old. Pursuing the process of selection that resulted in the choice of him in particular would involve trespassing in what, to a Westerner, is terra incognita, where belief, thought and action exist in a dimension of existence of which we are ignorant or maybe have merely forgotten.

According to Buddhist tradition every new Dalai Lama is a reincarnation of his predecessor, and when the Thirteenth died in 1933 a search was immediately instigated to find his reincarnation; oracles and learned lamas were consulted and certain signs observed. Strange cloud formations drifted across the heavens; the deceased, placed in the so-called Buddha position facing south, was found two days later facing east. This indicated that a search should be carried out to the east, and a delegation accordingly set forth, first to one of Tibet's sacred lakes, where the future could be revealed in the surface of the water. In this case a monastery was indicated, as well as a house with turquoise-colored tiles.

The delegation continued on its way, and found first the monastery and then the house, in the village of Takster in Eastern Tibet. It was the home of a crofter and his family, and they were asked if they had any children. They had a two-year-old son called Tenzin Gyatso. A number of inexplicable acts carried out by this boy convinced the delegation that they were at their journey's end, and that the Fourteenth Dalai Lama had been found.

Like so much else in the realm of religion this is not something we are asked to comprehend without reason: we encounter phenomena that belong to a reality different from our own, and to which we should respond not with an attempt at a rational explanation, but with reverent wonder.

Throughout its history Tibet has been a closed country, with little contact with the outside world. This is also true of modern times, and maybe explains why its leaders failed to attach due importance to formal de jure recognition of their country as an autonomous state. This, too, may be one of the reasons why the outside world did not feel under any obligation to support Tibt, when the country in 1950 and the years that followed was gradually occupied by the Chinese, who—in direct opposition to the Tibetans' own interpretation—claimed that Tibet had always been a part of China. In occupying the country the Chinese have, according to the conclusion reached by the International Commission of Jurists, been guilty of "the most pernicious crime that any individual or nation can be accused of, viz. a willful attempt to annihilate an entire people."

Meanwhile Tenzin Gyatso had by now reached the age of sixteen, and in the critical situation that now arose, he was charged with the task of playing the role of political leader to his people. Up till then the country had been ruled on his behalf by regents. He would have to assume the authority that the title of Dalai Lama involved, a boy of sixteen, without political experience, and with no education beyond his study of Buddhist lore, which he had absorbed throughout his upbringing. In his autobiography "My Land and My People," he has given us a vivid account of his rigorous apprenticeship at the hands of Tibetan lamas, and he declares that what he learnt was to prove no mean preparation for his allotted career, not least the political part of his work. It was on this basis he now developed the policy of non-violence with which he decided to confront the Chinese invaders. As a Buddhist monk it was his duty never to harm any living creature, but instead to show compassion to all life. If is maybe not to be wondered at that people so closely involved in what they call the world of reality should consider his philosophy somewhat remote from ordinary considerations of military strategy.

The policy of non-violence was also, of course, based on pragmatic considerations: a small nation of some six million souls, with no armed forces to speak of, faced one of the world's military super-powers. In a situation of this kind the non-violent approach was, in the opinion of the Dalai Lama, the only practicable one.

In accordance with this he made several attempts during the 1950s to negotiate with the Chinese. His aim was to arrive at a solution of the conflict that would be acceptable to both parties to the dispute, based on mutual respect and tolerance. To achieve this he staked all his authority as Dalai Lama to prevent any use of violence on the part of the Tibetans; and his authority proved decisive, for as the Dalai Lama he is, according to the Buddhist faith, more than a leader in the traditional sense: he symbolizes the whole nation. His very person is imbued with some of the attributes of a deity, which doubtless explains why his people, despite gross indignities and acute provocation, have to such a marked degree obeyed his wishes and abstained from the use of violence.

From his exile in India he now waged his unarmed struggle for his people with untiring patience. He has every justification for calling his autobiography ''My Land and My People,'' because the life of the Tibetans is in truth his life.

But political support from the outside world remained conspicuous by its absence, apart from a few rather toothless U.N. resolutions that were adopted in 1961 and 1965. Throughout the sixties and seventies the Dalai Lama was regarded as a pathetic figure from a distant past: his beautiful and well-meaning philosophy of peace was unfortunately out of place in this world.

There are several reasons for this. What has happened—and is still happening—in Tibet has become more generally known, and the community of nations has started to feel a sense of joint responsibility for the future of the Tibetan people. That their trials and tribulations have failed to break the spirit of the Tibetans is another reason; on the contrary their feeling of national pride and identity and their determination to survive have been enhanced, and these are expressed in massive demonstrations. Here, as in other parts of the world it is becoming increasingly obvious that problems cannot be solved by the use of brutal military power to crush peaceful demonstrations. In Tibet, as elsewhere, conflicts must be resolved politically through the medium of genuine negotiation.

For perfectly understandable reasons the policy of non-violence is often regarded as something negative, as a failure to formulate a well-considered strategy, as a lack of initiative and a tendency to evade the issue and adopt a passive attitude. But this is not so: the policy of non-violence is to a very high degree a well thought-out combat strategy. It demands single-minded and purposeful action, but one that eschews the use of force. Those who adopt this strategy are by no means shirking the issue: they manifest a moral courage which, when all is said and done, exceeds that of men who resort to arms. It is courage of this kind, together with an incredible measure of self-discipline, that has characterized the attitude of the Dalai Lama. His policy of non-violence too, has been carefully considered and determined. As he himself put it in April of last year, after a peaceful demonstration in Lhasa had been fired on by troops: "As I have explained on many occasions, non-violence is for us the only way. Quite patently in our case violence would be tantamount to suicide. For this reason, whether we like it or not, non-violence is the only approach, and the right one. We only need more patience and determination."

In 1987 the Dalai Lama submitted a peace plan for Tibet, the gist of which was that Tibet should be given the status of a "peace zone" on a par with what had been proposed for Nepal, a proposal which the Chinese in fact have supported. The plan also envisaged a halt to Chinese immigration to Tibet. This has proceeded on such a scale that there is a risk of the Tibetans becoming a minority in their own country. Not least interesting is the fact that the plan also contains measures for the conservation of Tibet's unique natural environment. Wholesale logging operations in the forests on the slopes of the Himalayas have resulted in catastrophic soil erosion, and are one of the causes of the flood disasters suffered by India and Bangladesh. The peace plan failed to initiate any negotiations with the Chinese, even though the discrepancies between the two sides were not particularly profound.

The Dalai Lama's willingness to compromise was expressed still more clearly in his address to the European Parliament on June the 15th last year, where he stated his readiness to abandon claims for full Tibetan independence. He acknowledged that China, as an Asian super-power, had strategic interests in Tibet, and was prepared to accept a Chinese military presence, at any rate until such time as a regional peace plan could be adopted. He also expressed his willingness to leave foreign policy and defence in the hands of the Chinese. In return the Tibetans should be granted the right to full internal autonomy. In his efforts to promote peace the Dalai Lama has shown that what he aims to achieve is not a power base at the expense of others. He claims no more for his people than what everybody— no doubt the Chinese themselves—recognize as elementary human rights. In a world in which suspicion and aggression have all too long characterized relations between peoples and nations, and where the only realistic policy has been reliance on the use of power, a new confession of faith is emerging, namely that the least realistic of all solutions to conflict is the consistent use of force. Modern weapons have in fact excluded such solutions.

The world has shrunk. Increasingly peoples and nations have grown dependent on one another. No one can any longer act entirely in his own interests. It is therefore imperative that we should accept mutual responsibility for all political, economic, and ecological problems.

In view of this, fewer and fewer people would venture to dismiss the Dalai Lama's philosophy as utopian: on the contrary, one would be increasingly justified in asserting that his gospel of non-violence is the truly realistic one, with most promise for the future. And this applies not only to Tibet but to each and every conflict. The future hopes of oppressed millions are today linked to the unarmed battalions, for they will win the peace: the justice of their demands, moreover, is now so clear and the moral strength of their struggle so indomitable that they can only temporarily be halted by force of arms.

In awarding the Peace Prize to H. H. the Dalai Lama we affirm our unstinting support for his work for peace, and for the unarmed masses on the march in many lands for liberty, peace and human dignity.

The Nobel Peace Prize Acceptance Speech
Oslo, Norway, December 10, 1989

Your Majesty, Members of the Nobel Committee, Brothers and Sisters:

I am very happy to be here with you today to receive the Nobel Prize for Peace. I feel honored, humbled and deeply moved that you should give this important prize to a simple monk from Tibet. I am no one special. But, I believe the prize is a recognition of the true value of altruism, love, compassion and non-violence which I try to practice, in accordance with the teachings of the Buddha and the great sages of India and Tibet.

I accept the prize with profound gratitude on behalf of the oppressed everywhere and for all those who struggle for freedom and work for world peace. I accept it as a tribute to the man who founded the modern tradition of non-violent action for change—Mahatma Gandhi—whose life taught and inspired me. And, of course, I accept it on behalf of the six million Tibetan people, my brave countrymen and women inside Tibet, who have suffered and continue to suffer so much. They confront a calculated and systematic strategy aimed at the destruction of their national and cultural identities. The prize reaffirms our conviction that with truth, courage and determination as our weapons, Tibet will be liberated.

No matter what part of the world we come from, we are all basically the same human beings. We all seek happiness and try to avoid suffering. We have the same basic human needs and concerns. All of us human beings want freedom and the right to determine our own destiny as individuals and as peoples. That is human nature. The great changes that are taking place everywhere in the world, from Eastern Europe to Africa are a clear indication of this.

In China the popular movement for democracy was crushed by brutal force in June this year. But I do not believe the demonstrations were in vain, because the spirit of freedom was rekindled among the Chinese people and China cannot escape the impact of this spirit of freedom sweeping many parts of the world. The brave students and their supporters showed the Chinese leadership and world the human face of that great nation.

Last week a number of Tibetans were once again sentenced to prison terms of up to nineteen years at a mass show trial, possibly intended to frighten the population before today's event. Their only "crime" was the expression of the widespread desire of Tibetans for the restoration of their beloved country's independence.

The suffering of our people during the past forty years of occupation is well documented. Ours has been a long struggle. We know our cause is just. Because violence can only breed more violence and suffering, our struggle must remain non-violent and free of hatred. We are trying to end the suffering of our people, not to inflict suffering upon others.

It is with this in mind that I proposed negotiations between Tibet and China on numerous occasions. In 1987, I made specific proposals in a five-point plan for the restoration of peace and human rights in Tibet. This included the conversion of the entire Tibetan plateau into a Zone of Ahimsa, a sanctuary of peace and non-violence where human beings and nature can live in peace and harmony.

Last year, I elaborated on that plan in Strasbourg, at the European Parliament. I believe the ideas I expressed on those occasions are both realistic and reasonable, although they have been criticized by some of my people as being too conciliatory. Unfortunately, China's leaders have not responded positively to the suggestions we have made, which included important concessions. If this continues we will be compelled to reconsider our position.

Any relationship between Tibet and China will have to be based on the principle of equality, respect, trust and mutual benefit. It will also have to be based on the principle which the wise rulers of Tibet and of China laid down in a treaty as early as 823 A.D., carved on the pillar which still stands today in front of the Jo-khang, Tibet's holiest shrine, in Lhasa, that "Tibetans will live happily in the great land of Tibet, and the Chinese will live happily in the great land of China."

As a Buddhist monk, my concern extends to all members of the human family and, indeed, to all sentient beings who suffer. I believe all suffering is caused by ignorance. People inflict pain on others in the selfish pursuit of their happiness or satisfaction. Yet true happiness comes from a sense of inner peace and contentment, which in turn must be achieved through the cultivation of altruism, of love and compassion and elimination of ignorance, selfishness and greed.

The problems we face today, violent conflicts, destruction of nature, poverty, hunger, and so on, are human created problems which can be resolved through human effort, understanding and the development of a sense of brotherhood and sisterhood. We need to cultivate a universal responsibility for one another and the planet we share. Although I have found my own Buddhist religion helpful in generating love and compassion, even for those we consider our enemies, I am convinced that everyone can develop a good heart and a sense of universal responsibility with or without religion.

With the ever-growing impact of science on our lives religion and spirituality have a greater role to play reminding us of our humanity. There is no contradiction between the two. Each gives us valuable insights into the other. Both science and the teachings of the Buddha tell us of the fundamental unity of all things. This understanding is crucial if we are to take positive and decisive action on the pressing global concern with the environment.

I believe all religions pursue the same goals, that of cultivating human goodness and bringing happiness to all human beings. Though the means might appear different the ends are the same.

As we enter the final decade of this century I am optimistic that the ancient values that have sustained mankind are today reaffirming themselves to prepare us for a kinder, happier twenty-first century.

I pray for all of us, oppressor and friend, that together we succeed in building a better world through human understanding and love, and that in doing so we may reduce the pain and suffering of all sentient beings.

Thank you.

His Holiness receiving the Nobel Peace Prize from Mr. Egil Aarvik, Chairman of the Norwegian Nobel Committee. *Photo: Dr. Jan Andersson*

His Holiness The Dalai Lama's Statement on the Use of the Nobel Peace Prize Money

I have decided to donate a portion of the prize money for the many who are facing starvation in various parts of the world; a portion of it for some of the leprosy programs in India; a portion of it to some existing institutions and programs working on peace; and finally, I would like to use a portion of it as seed money to eventually establish a Tibetan Foundation for Universal Responsibility.

This new foundation will implement projects according to Tibetan Buddhist principles to benefit people everywhere, focusing especially on assisting non-violent methods, on improving communication between religion and science, on securing human rights and democratic freedoms, and on conserving and restoring our precious Mother Earth.

I have deliberately added "Tibetan" to the foundation's name so that this will be one of the first truly Tibetan foundations established to act from the heart of the Tibetan people to do good and helpful things not only for their own country but for people throughout the world.

Old Tibet was a bit too isolated. The future Tibet will be

active to help those in need throughout the world, especially using our expertise in psychological, spiritual, and philosophical matters. Of course, many individuals, foundations and governments are already working in these areas, and many more will surely do so as the planetary crisis becomes more obvious and intense. But I believe that our Tibetan combination of spirituality and practicality will make a special contribution, in however modest a way. Once this foundation begins to work we hope to be able to show what a free Tibet can give to the world when its time has come.

Oslo, Norway
December 10, 1989

His Holiness delivering the 1989 Nobel Lecture.

Photo: Dr. Jan Andersson

December 11

THE NOBEL LECTURES

His Holiness with Mr. Egil Aarvik, Chairman of the Norwegian Nobel Committee. Mr. Gunner Stålsett is behind them.   *Photo: Dr. Jan Andersson*

Introductory Remarks by the Nobel Committee on the Occasion of the Nobel Lecture by His Holiness The Dalai Lama—December 11, 1989

Your Holiness, Excellencies, Ladies and Gentlemen:

It is an honor and a joy for the Norwegian Nobel Committee to welcome you to this special meeting with His Holiness the Fourteenth Dalai Lama. The only formal duty for a Nobel Peace Laureate is to present in a public lecture his or her reflections on the philosophy, ideas and struggles which have led to the award. This is an occasion for the laureate to express in a more coherent and comprehensive way those elements of a philosophy and peace strategy which have already been identified in numerous speeches, remarks and press conferences these hectic days in Oslo. We have come here to listen and to learn as one of the great spiritual leaders of our time will present to us his vision for a peaceful solution to conflicts.

Your Holiness, the awarding of the 1989 Nobel Peace Prize to you as the spiritual and national leader of the Tibetan people has been met with overwhelming positive reaction worldwide. It is in your own spirit that we have offered you the prize as an instrument for reconciliation. In your hands the Peace

Prize is an instrument for peace. In the official statement of the Nobel Committee, we have identified three specific elements in your peace philosophy: non-violent solution of international conflicts, the interrelatedness of social and individual human rights, and the critical need in our generation to face the threat of a global environmental disaster.

The focus of the prize this year is Tibet and the Tibetan people. But the significance of the message sent by this year's award is global. It addresses the future of minority nationalities in many nations, great and small. It raises the question of social welfare, education, and cultural and spiritual identity and integrity as vital for the survival of an ethnic minority. The message of Your Holiness as we are hearing it is, avoid violence, work for negotiated peaceful settlements, seek change without bloodshed, freedom without anarchy, express national pride without nationalistic feeling. From the ancient and venerable Buddhist tradition, you bring us the message of the importance of seeing mind and matter, humanity and nature as one. From the great wisdom of the past comes guidance for our common future. It is significant indeed, that the ecological issue has been put on the agenda of the Nobel Peace Prize Committee by a spiritual leader who combines rationality, humanism and religious tradition as a foundation for a moral response to the great challenges of the twentieth century. Your Holiness, I invite you to present the Nobel Peace Lecture of 1989.

The Nobel Peace Prize Lecture
Oslo, Norway

Brothers and Sisters:

It is an honor and pleasure to be among you today. I am really happy to see so many old friends who have come from different corners of the world, and to make new friends, whom I hope to meet again in the future. When I meet people in different parts of the world, I am always reminded that we are all basically alike: we are all human beings. Maybe we have different clothes, our skin is of a different color, or we speak different languages. This is on the surface. But basically, we are the same human beings. That is what binds us to each other. That is what makes it possible for us to understand each other and to develop friendship and closeness.

Thinking over what I might say today, I decided to share with you some of my thoughts concerning the common problems all of us face as members of the human family. Because we all share this small planet earth, we have to learn to live in harmony and peace with each other and with nature. That is not just a dream, but a necessity. We are dependent on each other in so many ways that we can no longer live in isolated communities and ignore what is happening outside those communities. We need to help each other when we have difficulties, and we must share the good fortune that we enjoy. I speak to you as just another human being, as a simple monk. If you find what I say useful, then I hope you will try to practice it. I also wish to share with you today my feelings concerning the plight and aspirations of the people of Tibet. The Nobel Prize is a prize they well deserve for their courage and unfailing determination during the past forty years of foreign occupation. As a free spokesman for my captive countrymen and -women, I feel it is my duty to speak out on their behalf. I speak not with a feeling of anger or hatred towards those who are responsible for the immense suffering of our people and the destruction of our land, homes and culture. They too are human beings who struggle to find happiness and deserve our compassion. I speak to inform you of the sad situation in my country today and of the aspirations of my people, because in our struggle for freedom, truth is the only weapon we possess.

The realization that we are all basically the same human beings, who seek happiness and try to avoid suffering, is very helpful in developing a sense of brotherhood and sisterhood—a warm feeling of love and compassion for others. This, in turn, is essential if we are to survive in this ever-shrinking world we live in. For if we each selfishly pursue only what we believe to be in our own interest, without caring about the needs of others, we not only may end up harming others but also ourselves. This fact has become very clear during the course of this century. We know that to wage a nuclear war today, for example, would be a form of suicide; or that to pollute the air or the oceans, in order to achieve some short-term benefit, would be to destroy the very basis for our survival. As individuals and nations are becoming increasingly interdependent we have no other choice than to develop what I call a sense of universal responsibility.

Today, we are truly a global family. What happens in one part of the world may affect us all. This, of course, is not only true of the negative things that happen, but is equally valid for the positive developments. We not only know what happens elsewhere, thanks to the extraordinary modern communications technology, we are also directly affected by events that occur far away. We feel a sense of sadness when children are starving in Eastern Africa. Similarly, we feel a sense of joy when a family is reunited after decades of separation by the Berlin Wall. Our crops and livestock are contaminated and our health and livelihood threatened when a nuclear accident happens miles away in another country. Our own security is enhanced when peace breaks out between warring parties in other continents.

But war or peace; the destruction or the protection of nature; the violation or promotion of human rights and democratic freedoms; poverty or material well being; the lack of moral and spiritual values or their existence and development; and the breakdown or development of human understanding, are not isolated phenomena that can be analyzed and tackled independently of one another. In fact, they are very much interrelated at all levels and need to be approached with that understanding.

Peace, in the sense of the absence of war, is of little value to someone who is dying of hunger or cold. It will not remove the pain of torture inflicted on a prisoner of conscience. It does not comfort those who have lost their loved ones in floods caused by senseless deforestation in a neighboring country. Peace can only last where human rights are respected, where the people are fed, and where individuals and nations are free. True peace with ourselves and with the world around us can only be achieved through the development of mental peace. The other phenomena mentioned above are similarly interrelated. Thus, for example, we see that a clean environment, wealth or democracy mean little in the face of war, especially nuclear war, and that material development is not sufficient to ensure human happiness.

Material progress is of course important for human advancement. In Tibet, we paid much too little attention to technological and economic development, and today we realize that this was a mistake. At the same time, material development without spiritual development can also cause serious problems. In some countries too much attention is paid to external things and very little importance is given to inner development. I believe both are important and must be developed side by side so as to achieve a good balance between them. Tibetans are always described by foreign visitors as being a happy, jovial people. This is part of our national character, formed by cultural and religious values that stress the importance of mental peace through the generation of love and kindness to all other living sentient beings, both human and animal. Inner peace is the key: if you have inner peace, the external problems do not affect your deep sense of peace and tranquility. In that state of mind you can deal with situations with calmness and reason, while keeping your inner happiness. That is very important. Without this inner peace, no matter how comfortable your life is materially, you may still be worried, disturbed or unhappy because of circumstances.

Clearly, it is of great importance, therefore, to understand the interrelationship among these and other phenomena, and to approach and attempt to solve problems in a balanced way that takes these different aspects into consideration. Of course it is not easy. But it is of little benefit to try to solve one problem if doing so creates an equally serious new one. So really we have no alternative: we must develop a sense of universal responsibility not only in the geographic sense, but also in respect to the different issues that confront our planet.

Responsibility does not only lie with the leaders of our countries or with those who have been appointed or elected to do a particular job. It lies with each of us individually. Peace, for example, starts within each one of us. When we have inner peace, we can be at peace with those around us. When our community is in a state of peace, it can share that peace with neighboring communities, and so on. When we feel love and kindness towards others, it not only makes others feel loved and cared for, but it helps us also to develop inner happiness and peace. And there are ways in which we can consciously work to develop feelings of love and kindness. For some of us, the most effective way to do so is through religious practice. For others it may be non-religious practices. What is important is that we each make a sincere effort to take seriously our responsibility for each other and for the natural environment.

I am very encouraged by the developments which are taking place around us. After the young people of many countries, particularly in northern Europe, have repeatedly called for an end to the dangerous destruction of the environment which was being conducted in the name of economic development, the world's political leaders are now starting to take meaningful steps to address this problem. The report to the United Nations Secretary General by the World Commission on the Environment and Development (the Brundtland report) was an important step in educating governments on the urgency of the issue. Serious efforts to bring peace to war-torn zones and to implement the right to self-determination of some peoples have resulted in the withdrawal of Soviet troops from Afghanistan and the establishment of independent Namibia. Through persistent non-violent popular efforts dramatic changes, bringing many countries closer to real democracy, have occurred in many places, from Manila in the Philippines to Berlin in East Germany. With the Cold War era apparently drawing to a close, people everywhere live with renewed hope. Sadly, the courageous efforts of the Chinese people to bring similar change to their country was brutally crushed last June. But their efforts too are a source of hope. The military might has not extinguished the desire for freedom and the determination of the Chinese people to achieve it. I particularly admire the fact that these young people, who have been taught that "power grows from the barrel of the gun," chose, instead, to use non-violence as their weapon.

What these positive changes indicate is that reason, courage, determination, and the inextinguishable desire for freedom can ultimately win. In the struggle between forces of war, violence and oppression on the one hand, and peace, reason and freedom on the other, the latter are gaining the upper hand. This realization fills us Tibetans with hope that some day we too will once again be free.

The awarding of the Nobel Prize to me, a simple monk from far-away Tibet, here in Norway, also fills us Tibetans with hope. It means that, despite the fact that we have not drawn attention to our plight by means of violence, we have not been forgotten. It also means that the values we cherish, in particular our respect for all forms of life and the belief in the power of truth, are today recognized and encouraged. It is also a tribute to my mentor, Mahatma Gandhi, whose example is an inspiration to so many of us. This year's award is an indication that this sense of universal responsibility is developing. I am deeply touched by the sincere concern shown by so many people in this part of the world for the suffering of the people of Tibet. That is a source of hope not only for us Tibetans, but for all oppressed peoples.

As you know, Tibet has, for forty years, been under foreign occupation. Today, more than a quarter of a million Chinese troops are stationed in Tibet. Some sources estimate the occupation army to be twice this strength. During this time, Tibetans have been deprived of their most basic human rights, including the right to life, movement, speech, worship, only to mention a few. More than one sixth of Tibet's population of six million died as a direct result of the Chinese invasion and occupation. Even before the Cultural Revolution started, many of Tibet's monsteries, temples and historic buildings were destroyed. Almost everything that remained was destroyed during the Cultural Revolution. I do not wish to dwell on this point, which is well documented. What is important to realize, however, is that despite the limited freedom granted after 1979 to rebuild parts of some monasteries and other such tokens of liberalization, the fundamental human rights of the Tibetan people are still today being systematically violated. In recent months this bad situation has become even worse.

If it were not for our community in exile, so generously sheltered and supported by the government and people of India and helped by organizations and individuals from many parts of the world, our nation would today be little more than a shattered remnant of a people. Our culture, religion and national identity would have been effectively eliminated. As it is, we have built schools and monasteries in exile and have created democratic institutions to serve our people and preserve the seeds of our civilization. With this experience, we intend to implement full democracy in a future free Tibet. Thus, as we develop our community in exile on modern lines, we also cherish and preserve our own identity and culture and bring hope to millions of our countrymen and -women in Tibet.

The issue of most urgent concern at this time is the massive influx of Chinese settlers into Tibet. Although in the first decades of occupation a considerable number of Chinese were transferred into the eastern parts of Tibet—in the Tibetan provinces of Amdo (Chinghai) and Kham (most of which has been annexed by the neighboring Chinese province)—since 1983 an unprecedented number of Chinese have been encouraged by their government to migrate to all parts of Tibet, including central and western Tibet (which the PRC refers to as the so-called Tibet Autonomous Region). Tibetans are rapidly being reduced to an insignificant minority in their own country. This development, which threatens the very survival of the Tibetan nation, its culture and spiritual heritage, can still be stopped and reversed. But this must be done now, before it is too late.

The new cycle of protest and violent repression, which started in Tibet in September of 1987 and culminated in the imposition of martial law in the capital, Lhasa, in March of this year, was in large part a reaction to this tremendous Chinese influx. Information reaching us in exile indicates that the protest marches and other peaceful forms of protest are continuing in Lhasa and a number of other places in Tibet despite the severe punishment and inhumane treatment given to Tibetans detained for expressing their grievances. The number of Tibetans killed by security forces during the protest in March and of those who died in detention afterwards is not known but is believed to be more than two hundred. Thousands have been detained or arrested and imprisoned, and torture is commonplace.

It was against the background of this worsening situation and in order to prevent further bloodshed, that I proposed what is generally referred to as the Five Point Peace Plan for the restoration of peace and human rights in Tibet. I elaborated on the plan in a speech in Strasbourg last year. I believe the plan provides a reasonable and realistic framework for negotiations with the People's Republic of China. So far, however, China's leaders have been unwilling to respond constructively. The brutal supression of the Chinese democracy movement in June of this year, however, reinforced my view that any settlement of the Tibetan question will only be meaningful if it is supported by adequate international guarantees.

The Five Point Peace Plan addresses the principal and inter-related issues, which I referred to in the first part of this lecture. It calls for (1) Transformation of the whole of Tibet, including the eastern provinces of Kham and Amdo, into a zone of Ahimsa (non-violence); (2) Abandonment of China's population transfer policy; (3) Respect for the Tibetan people's fundamental human rights and democratic freedoms; (4) Restoration and protection of Tibet's natural environment; and (5) Commencement of earnest negotiations on the future status of Tibet and of relations between the Tibetan and Chinese peoples. In the Strasbourg address I proposed that Tibet become a fully self-governing democratic political entity.

I would like to take this opportunity to explain the Zone of Ahimsa or peace sanctuary concept, which is the central element of the Five Point Peace Plan. I am convinced that it is of great importance not only for Tibet, but for peace and stability in Asia.

It is my dream that the entire Tibetan plateau should become a free refuge where humanity and nature can live in peace and in harmonious balance. It would be a place where people from all over the world could come to seek the true meaning of peace within themselves, away from the tensions and pressures of much of the rest of the world. Tibet could indeed become a creative center for the promotion and development of peace.

The following are key elements of the proposed Zone of Ahimsa:

—the entire Tibetan plateau would be demilitarized;
—the manufacture, testing, and stockpiling of nuclear weapons and other armaments on the Tibetan plateau would be prohibited;

—the Tibetan plateau would be transformed into the world's largest natural park or biosphere. Strict laws would be enforced to protect wildlife and plant life; the exploitation of natural resources would be carefully regulated so as not to damage relevant ecosystems; and a policy of sustainable development would be adopted in populated areas;

—the manufacture and use of nuclear power and other technologies which produce hazardous waste would be prohibited;

—national resources and policy would be directed towards the active promotion of peace and environmental protection. Organizations dedicated to the furtherance of peace and to the protection of all forms of life would find a hospitable home in Tibet;

—the establishment of international and regional organizations for the promotion and protection of human rights would be encouraged in Tibet.

Tibet's height and size (the size of the European Community), as well as its unique history and profound spiritual heritage make it ideally suited to fulfill the role of a sanctuary of peace in the strategic heart of Asia. It would also be in keeping with Tibet's historical role as a peaceful Buddhist nation and buffer region separating the Asian continent's great and often rival powers.

In order to reduce existing tensions in Asia, the President of the Soviet Union, Mr. Gorbachev, proposed the demilitarization of Soviet-Chinese borders and their transformation into a "frontier of peace and good-neighborliness." The Nepal government had earlier proposed that the Himalayan country of Nepal, bordering on Tibet, should become a zone of peace, although that proposal did not include demilitarization of the country.

For the stability and peace of Asia, it is essential to create peace zones to separate the continent's biggest powers and potential adversaries. President Gorbachev's proposal, which also included a complete Soviet troop withdrawal from Mongolia, would help to reduce tension and the potential for confrontation between the Soviet Union and China. A true peace zone must, clearly, also be created to separate the world's two most populous states, China and India.

The establishment of the Zone of Ahimsa would require the withdrawal of troops and military installations from Tibet, which would enable India and Nepal also to withdraw troops and military installations from the Himalayan regions bordering Tibet. This would have to be achieved by international agreements. It would be in the best interest of all states in Asia, particularly China and India, as it would enhance their security, while reducing the economic burden of maintaining high troop concentrations in remote areas.

Tibet would not be the first strategic area to be demilitarized. Parts of the Sinai peninsula, the Egyptian territory separating Israel and Egypt, have been demilitarized for some time. Of course, Costa Rica is the best example of an entirely demilitarized country.

Tibet would also not be the first area to be turned into a natural preserve or biosphere. Many parks have been created throughout the world. Some very strategic areas have been turned into natural "peace parks." Two examples are the La Amistad park, on the Cost Rica-Panama border and the Si A Paz project on the Costa Rica-Nicaragua border.

When I visited Costa Rica earlier this year, I saw how a country can develop successfully without an army, to become a stable democracy committed to peace and the protection of the natural environment. This confirmed my belief that my vision of Tibet in the future is a realistic plan, not merely a dream.

Let me end with a personal note of thanks to all of you and our friends who are not here today. The concern and support which you have expressed for the plight of the Tibetans has touched us all greatly, and continues to give us courage to struggle for freedom and justice; not through the use of arms, but with the powerful weapons of truth and determination. I know that I speak on behalf of all the people of Tibet when I thank you and ask you not to forget Tibet at this critical time in our country's history. We too hope to contribute to the development of a more peaceful, more humane and more beautiful world. A future free Tibet will seek to help those in need throughout the world, to protect nature, and to promote peace. I believe that our Tibetan ability to combine spiritual qualities with a realistic and practical attitude enables us to make a special contribution in however modest a way. This is my hope and prayer.

In conclusion, let me share with you a short prayer which gives me great inspiration and determination:

For as long as space endures,
And for as long as living beings remain,
Until then may I, too, abide
To dispel the misery of the world.

Thank you.

The Nobel Evening Address
Oslo, Norway

Brothers and Sisters:

It is a great honor to come to this place and to share some of my thoughts with you. Although I have written a speech, it has already been circulated [see Chapter 1]. You know, some of my friends told me it is better to speak in Tibetan and have it translated into English; some say it is better to read my English statement; and some say it is better to speak directly with my broken English. I don't know. Yesterday, I tried my best to be formal but today I feel more free, so I will speak informally. In any case, the main points of my speech are on paper for you to see.

I think it advisable to summarize some of the points that I will consider. I usually discuss three main topics. Firstly, as a human being, as a citizen of the world, every human being has a responsibility for the planet. Secondly, as a Buddhist monk, I have a special connection with the spiritual world. I try to contribute something in that field. Thirdly, as a Tibetan I have a responsibility to the fate of the Tibetan nation. On behalf of these unfortunate people, I will speak briefly about their concerns.

So now, firstly, what is the purpose of life for a human being? I believe that happiness is the purpose of life. Whether or not there is a purpose to the existence of the universe or galaxies, I don't know. In any case, the fact is that we are here on this planet with other human beings. Then, since every human being wants happiness and does not want suffering, it is clear that this desire does not come from training, or from some ideology. It is something natural. Therefore, I consider that the attainment of happiness, peace, and joy is the purpose of life. Therefore, it is very important to investigate what are happiness and satisfaction and what are their causes.

I think that there is a mental factor as well as a physical factor. Both are very important. If we compare these two things, the mental factor is more important, superior to the physical factor. This we can know through our daily life. Since the mental factor is more important, we have to give serious thought to inner qualities.

Then, I believe compassion and love are necessary in order for us to obtain happiness or tranquility. These mental factors are key. I think they are the basic source. What is compassion? From the Buddhist viewpoint there are different varieties of compassion. The basic meaning of compassion is not just a feeling of closeness, or just a feeling of pity. Rather, I think that with genuine compassion we not only feel the pains and suffering of others but we also have a feeling of determination to overcome that suffering. One aspect of compassion is some kind of determination and responsibility. Therefore, compassion brings us tranquility and also inner strength. Inner strength is the ultimate source of success.

When we face some problem, a lot depends on the personal attitude towards that problem or tragedy. In some cases, when one faces the difficulty, one loses one's hope and becomes discouraged and then ends up depressed. On the other hand, if one has a certain mental attitude, then tragedy and suffering bring one more energy, more determination.

Usually, I tell our generation we are born during the darkest period in our long history. There is a big challenge. It is very unfortunate. But if there is a challenge then there is an oppor-

tunity to face it, an opportunity to demonstrate our will and
our determination. So from that viewpoint I think that our
generation is fortunate. These things depend on inner qualities, inner strength. Compassion is very gentle, very peaceful,
and soft in nature, not harsh. You cannot destroy it easily as
it is very powerful. Therefore, compassion is very important and
useful.

Then, again, if we look at human nature, love and compassion are the foundation of human existence. According to some
scientists, the foetus has feeling in the mother's womb and is
affected by the mother's mental state. Then the few weeks after birth are crucial for the enlarging of the brain of the child.
During that period, the mother's physical touch is the greatest
factor for the healthy development of the brain. This shows that
the physical needs some affection to develop properly.

When we are born, our first action is sucking milk from the
mother. Of course, the child may not know about compassion
and love, but the natural feeling is one of closeness toward the
object that gives the milk. If the mother is angry or has ill feeling, the milk may not come fully. This shows that from our
first day as human beings the effect of compassion is crucial.

If unpleasant things happen in our daily life, we immediately
pay attention to them but do not notice other pleasant things.
We experience these as normal or usual. This shows that compassion and affection are part of human nature.

Compassion or love has different levels; some are more mixed
than others with desire or attachment. For example, parents'
attitudes toward their children contain a mixture of desire and
attachment with compassion. The love and compassion between
husband and wife—especially at the beginning of marriage when
they don't know the deep nature of each other—are on a su-
perficial level. As soon as the attitude of one partner changes,
the attitude of the other becomes opposite to what it was. That
kind of love and compassion is more of the nature of attachment. Attachment means some kind of feeling of closeness
projected by oneself. In reality, the other side may be very negative, but due to one's own mental attachment and projection,

it appears as something nice. Furthermore, attachment causes one to exaggerate a small good quality and make it appear 100% beautiful or 100% positive. As soon as the mental attitudes change, that picture completely changes. Therefore, that kind of love and compassion is, rather, attachment.

Another kind of love and compassion is not based on something appearing beautiful or nice, but based on the fact that the other person, just like oneself, wants happiness and does not want suffering and indeed has every right to be happy and to overcome suffering. On such a basis, we feel a sense of responsibility, a sense of closeness toward that being. That is true compassion. This is because the compassion is based on reason, not just on emotional feeling. As a consequence, it does not matter what the other's attitude is, whether negative or positive. What matters is that it is a human being, a sentient being that has the experience of pain and pleasure. There is no reason not to feel compassion so long as it is a sentient being.

The kinds of compassion at the first level are mixed, interrelated. Some people have the view that some individuals have a very negative, cruel attitude towards others. These kinds of individuals appear to have no compassion in their minds. But I feel that these people do have the seed of compassion. The reason for this is that even these people very much appreciate it when someone else shows them affection. A capacity to appreciate other people's affection means that in their deep mind there is the seed of compassion.

Compassion and love are not man-made. Ideology is man-made, but these things are produced by nature. It is important to recognize natural qualities, especially when we face a problem and fail to find a solution. For example, I feel that the Chinese leaders face a problem which is in part due to their own ideology, their own system. But when they try to solve that problem through their own ideology, then they fail to tackle that problem. In religious business, sometimes even due to religion, we create a problem. If we try to solve that problem using religious methods, it is quite certain that we will not succeed. So I feel that when we face those kind of problems, it is important to return to our basic human quality. Then I think we will find that solutions come easier. Therefore, I usually say that the best way to solve human problems is with human understanding.

It is very important to recognize the basic nature of humanity and the value of human qualties. Whether one is educated or uneducated, rich or poor, or belongs to this nation or that nation, this religion or that religion, this ideology or that ideology, is secondary and doesn't matter. When we return to this basis, all people are the same. Then we can truly say the words brother, sister; then they are not just nice words—they have some meaning. That kind of motivation automatically builds the practice of kindness. This gives us inner strength.

What is my purpose in life, what is my responsibility? Whether I like it or not, I am on this planet, and it is far better to do something for humanity. So you see that compassion is the seed or basis. If we take care to foster compassion, we will see that it brings the other good human qualities. The topic of compassion is not at all religious business; it is very important to know that it is human business, that it is a question of human survival, that is not a question of human luxury. I might say that religion is a kind of luxury. If you have religion, that is good. But it is clear that even without religion we can manage. However, without these basic human qualities we cannot survive. It is a question of our own peace and mental stability.

Next, let us talk about the human being as a social animal. Even if we do not like other people, we have to live together. Natural law is such that even bees and other animals have to live together in cooperation. I am attracted to bees because I like honey—it is really delicious. Their product is something that we cannot produce, very beautiful, isn't it? I exploit them too much, I think. Even these insects have certain responsibilities, they work together very nicely. They have no constitution, they have no law, no police, nothing, but they work together effectively. This is because of nature. Similarly, each part of a flower is not arranged by humans but by nature. The force of nature is something remarkable. We human beings, we have constitutions, we have law, we have a police force, we have religion, we have many things. But in actual practice, I think that we are behind those small insects.

Sometimes civilization brings good progress, but we become too involved with this progress and neglect or forget about our basic nature. Every development in human society should take place on the basis of the foundation of the human nature. If we lose that basic foundation, there is no point in such developments taking place.

In cooperation, working together, the key thing is the sense of responsibility. But this cannot be developed by force as has been attempted in eastern Europe and in China. There a tremendous effort has to be made to develop in the mind of every individual human being a sense of responsibility, a concern for the common interest rather than the individual interest. They aim their education, their ideology, their efforts to brainwash, at this. But their means are abstract, and the sense of responsibility cannot develop. The genuine sense of responsibility will develop only through compassion and altruism.

The modern economy has no national boundaries. When we talk about ecology, the environment, when we are concerned about the ozone layer, one individual, one society, one country cannot solve these problems. We must work together. Humanity needs more genuine cooperation. The foundation for the development of good relations with one another is altruism, compassion, and forgiveness. For small arguments to remain limited, in the human circle the best method is forgiveness. Altruism and forgiveness are the basis for bringing humanity together. Then no conflict, no matter how serious, will go beyond the bounds of what is truly human.

I will tell you something. I love friends, I want more friends. I love smiles. That is a fact. How to develop smiles? There are a variety of smiles. Some smiles are sarcastic. Some smiles are artificial—diplomatic smiles. These smiles do not produce satisfaction, but rather fear or suspicion. But a genuine smile gives us hope, freshness. If we want a genuine smile, then first we must produce the basis for a smile to come. On every level of human life, compassion is the key thing.

Now, on the question of violence and non-violence. There are many different levels of violence and non-violence. On the basis of external action, it is difficult distinguish whether an action is violent or non-violent. Basically, it depends on the motivation behind the action. If the motivation is negative, even though the external appearance may be very smooth and gentle, in a deeper sense the action is very violent. On the contrary, harsh actions and words done with a sincere, positive motivation are essentially non-violent. In other words, violence is a destructive power. Non-violence is constructive.

When the days become longer and there is more sunshine, the grass becomes fresh and, consequently, we feel very happy. On the other hand, in autumn, one leaf falls down and another leaf falls down. These beautiful plants become as if dead and we do not feel very happy. Why? I think it is because deep down our human nature likes construction, and does not like destruction. Naturally, every action which is destructive is against human nature. Constructiveness is the human way. Therefore, I think that in terms of basic human feeling, violence is not good. Non-violence is the only way.

Practically speaking, through violence we may achieve something, but at the expense of someone else's welfare. That way, although we may solve one problem, we simultaneously seed a new problem. The best way to solve problems is through human understanding, mutual respect. On one side make some concessions; on the other side take serious consideration about the problem. There may not be complete satisfaction, but something happens. At least future danger is avoided. Non-violence is very safe.

Before my first visit to Europe in 1973, I had felt the importance of compassion, altruism. On many occasions I expressed the importance of the sense of universal responsibility. Sometimes during this period, some people felt that the Dalai Lama's idea was a bit unrealistic. Unfortunately, in the Western world Gandhian non-violence is seen as passive resistance more suitable to the East. The Westerners are very active, demanding immediate results, even in the course of daily life. But today the actual situation teaches non-violence to people. The movement for freedom is non-violent. These recent events reconfirm to me that non-violence is much closer to human nature.

Again, if there are sound reasons or bases for the points you demand, then there is no need to use violence. On the other hand, when there is no sound reason that concessions should be made to you but mainly your own desire, then reason cannot work and you have to rely on force. Thus, using force is not a sign of strength but rather a sign of weakness. Even in daily human contact, if we talk seriously, using reasons, there is no need to feel anger. We can argue the points. When we fail to prove with reason, then anger comes. When reason ends, then anger begins. Therefore, anger is a sign of weakness.

In this, the second part of my talk, I speak as a Buddhist monk. As a result of more contact with people from other traditions, as time passes I have firmed my conviction that all religions can work together despite fundamental differences in philosophy. Every religion aims at serving humanity. Therefore, it is possible for the various religions to work together to serve humanity and contribute to world peace. So, during these last few years, at every opportunity I try to develop closer relations with other religions.

Buddhism does not accept a theory of God, or a Creator. According to Buddhism, one's own actions are the creator, ultimately. Some people say that, from a certain angle, Buddhism is not a religion but rather a science of mind. Religion has much involvement with faith. Sometimes it seems that there is quite a distance between a way of thinking based on faith and one entirely based on experiment, remaining sceptical. Unless you find something through investigation, you do not want to accept it as fact. From one viewpoint, Buddhism is a religion, from another viewpoint Buddhism is a science of mind and not a religion. Buddhism can be a bridge between these two sides. Therefore, with this conviction I try to have closer ties with scientists, mainly in the fields of cosmology, psychology, neurobiology, physics. In these fields there are insights to share, and to a certain extent we can work together.

Thirdly, I will speak on the Tibetan problem. One of the crucial, serious situations is the Chinese population transfer into Tibet. If the present situation continues for another ten or fifteen years, the Tibetans will be an insignificant minority in their own land, a situation similar to that in inner Mongolia. There the native population is around three million and the Chinese population is around ten million. In East Turkestan, the Chinese population is increasing daily. In Tibet, the native population is six million, whereas the Chinese population is already around seven and one-half million. This is really a serious matter.

In order to develop a closer understanding and harmony between the Chinese and Tibetans—the Chinese call it the unity of the motherland—the first thing necessary to provide the basis for the development of mutual respect is demilitarization, first to limit the number of Chinese soldiers and eventually to remove them altogether. This is crucial. Also, for the purposes of peace in that region, peace and genuine friendship between India and China, the two most populated nations, it is very essential to reduce military forces on both sides of the Himalayan range. For this reason, one point that I have made is that eventually Tibet should be a zone of ahimsa, a zone of non-violence.

Already there are clear indications of nuclear dumping in Tibet and of factories where nuclear weapons are produced. This is a serious matter. Also, there is deforestation, which is very dangerous for the environment. Respect for human rights is also necessary. These are the points I expressed in my Five-Point Peace Plan. These are crucial matters.

We are passing through a most difficult period. I am very encouraged by your warm expression and by the Nobel Peace Prize. I thank you from the depth of my heart.

Concluding Remarks by the Nobel Committee on the Occasion of the Nobel Lecture by His Holiness The Dalai Lama—December 11, 1989

Your Holiness, the best way for us to express our appreciation is to do it in the way you have greeted us, this way (hands pressed together), and you will find many Norwegians appreciating that language which you have taught us during these days. You have also opened to us the mysteries of the East, you have opened in this lecture the door to the wisdom of the East. As a Buddhist monk you remind us of a western monk, Francis of Assisi, who also used examples of everyday life to draw the conclusions which are important for the big matters of life. You have also shown us that the big matters of life are those which are related to compassion, which is not something soft: it is determination, it is persistence, it is a matter which carries hope about victory. You have changed this formal hall of lecture into a dialogue which has gone on in our minds and in our hearts, and we wish to thank you for that. We want this dialogue to continue as we accompany you in your further work to liberate your people. To provide a situation where human dignity, respect for human rights and freedom characterize the lives of millions who are now repressed. Thank you for coming, thank you for sharing in this particular way with us your thoughts and your wisdom. We wish you success as you continue to share with the Norwegian people during the next few days.

APPENDICES

Human Rights in Tibet Is Not An Internal Affair of China

by the U.S. Ambassador to the United Nations, Jeane J. Kirkpatrick

Last December 10, in Beijing, International Human Rights Day was celebrated with speeches, conferences and public marches. The same day, in Lhasa, Tibet's capital city, unarmed monks and nuns gathered in non-violent protest of Chinese oppression. The protest ended when Chinese police arrived and opened fire.

Recent days have seen more violence in Tibet. Again led by monks and nuns, Tibetans demanded independence from Chinese rule. Again Chinese police fired into crowds of demonstrators. Since March 5, according to the official China News Agency, at least twelve people have been killed and more than one hundred wounded in clashes between protestors and the police. Unofficial accounts say the toll is much higher.

Numerous observers, even a respected U.S. diplomat, have expressed surprise over the Chinese actions in Tibet. But, the surprise is that they're surprised. The recent clashes are only the latest of a string of abuses Tibetans have had to silently endure. Over the last thirty years the Tibetan plight has been among the most overlooked and underreported human rights abuses in the world. The Chinese have done everything they can to keep it that way, banning journalists and tourists from the Himalayan region—whenever anti-Chinese unrest has surfaced.

It is time the veil of secrecy be lifted. We in the West have a moral obligation to express our profound disapproval. Silence can only be considered as complicity. The catalogue of human rights abuses and cultural genocide Tibetans have suffered is deeply disturbing. Consider this:

- Since 1950, more than one million people have died as a direct result of the Chinese occupation, and more than one hundred thousand Tibetans fled to India and Nepal.
- More than six thousand monasteries have been razed and their monks defrocked and jailed.
- Thousands of Tibetan women have been victims of forced abortion and sterilization.
- Since 1987, some five thousand Tibetans have been arrested as political prisoners. Half are women and children.

The Chinese attitude toward the issue of human rights in Tibet has remained constant: it is an internal affair and not the concern of the rest of the world. Just two weeks ago, Chinese officials told President Bush, firmly but courteously, that this issue was not a concern of the United States. But human rights are an international concern, and violation of those rights should never be allowed to be hidden behind the pretext of internal affairs. The more that a government tries to repress information, the more important it is that others speak up.

In this century alone, more people have died at the hands of their own governments than in war. They have died in Pol Pot's murderous "utopia," Stalin's gulag, Hitler's final solution, the man-made famine in the Ukraine, and China's cultural revolution. Conservative estimates say ten million have died as a result of these massive human rights violations. To look away in the face of these atrocities is an act of moral cowardice. It is also the surest way to ensure their continuation.

Some have wondered why, during a time when China has been making progress in its relationship with Hong Kong and Taiwan, it would be so repressive in Tibet. The answer, perhaps, is that the Chinese thought no one would care. China's human rights abuses have been going on for three decades with little outcry from the international community. The last time the U.N. called for an end to human rights violations in Tibet was more than twenty years ago.

In its defense China says steps have been taken to modernize Tibet. It is true. Roads have been built, but these have been used mostly for moving the large occupation army. There are more jobs, but these are mostly for the Chinese living there. There are more power lines, yet these often by-pass Tibetan villages. There are questions as to how much this modernization benefits Tibetans.

Of course, we don't know if pressure from the world community, media, and governments will help improve China's human rights policy with regard to Tibet. Then again, it might help. Anatoly Shcharansky was freed from a Soviet gulag only through the efforts of his wife, Avital. For years, she was a tireless one-woman human rights campaign. She wouldn't let world governments or the media forget her husband, until he was released from prison.

History has shown us that silence only encourages human rights abusers. It is our responsibility, as people who enjoy the right of free expression, to speak out against Chinese abuses in Tibet. Maybe then the Chinese, in their effort to modernize, will build rights as well as roads.

[Adapted from Ambassador Kirkpatrick's speech delivered at Columbia University on March 5, 1989.]

Report From Tibet
"New Crackdown Follows Celebrations in Lhasa"
The Washington Post, December 21, 1989

LHASA, Tibet—The awarding of the Nobel Peace Prize to the Dalai Lama, Tibet's exiled spiritual and political leader, has increased tensions between China's Communist rulers and Tibetans and led to a renewed campaign of arrests, surveillance and political reeducation aimed at wiping out nationalist sentiment here, according to Tibetan and Chinese sources.

When news of the award began reaching here over All India Radio after it was announced Oct. 5, Tibetans flocked to holy parks and temples to rejoice and offer prayers of thanksgiving, said the sources, who refused to be identified for fear of government reprisals. In Lhasa, the religious center of Tibet, hundreds of pilgrims converged on the Norbulinka, the Dalai Lama's former summer palace, to sing, dance and drink barley beer.

The Dalai Lama headed Tibet's Buddhist theocracy until China forcibly annexed the area in 1950. When Chinese troops suppressed a nationalist uprising in 1959, the Dalai Lama fled to India and formed the Tibetan government in exile. Most of Tibet's monasteries were destroyed over the next 20 years, and nearly all monks were imprisoned or sent to labor camps.

A brief period of liberalization in Communist Party policies in the 1980s unleashed outbreaks of anti-Chinese protests in the region. Between September 1987 and March 1989, security or military forces in Tibet opened fire on non-violent demonstrators at least four times, according to foreign witnesses.

When police opened fire on protesters last March 5, three days of riots followed, according to foreign witnesses and Western press accounts. Medical workers interviewed recently in Lhasa said more than 200 Tibetans were killed—many more than previously reported—by police or troops during the turmoil. Since then, Lhasa, Tibet's capital, has been under martial law.

An estimated 10,000 People's Liberation Army troops now stand sentinel over the city's estimated 50,000 Tibetans, according to a Chinese official with military contacts. Soldiers are camped outside or within striking range of all monasteries, temples and nunneries in the capital, including the Jokhang Temple, the holiest of Tibet's Buddhist temples.

Lhasa's jails now hold more than 680 Tibetans accused of involvement in pro-independence activities, said Tibetans and Chinese officials. Almost half of these are monks, nuns and novices 13 and older. Prison officials routinely employ torture, including beatings and starvation, to extract confessions and information about pro-independence activists, said former detainees interviewed in Lhasa.

Martial-law troops, most of whom are Chinese and do not speak Tibetan, initially tolerated the festivities honoring the Dalai Lama's Nobel Prize. "We told the soldiers we were celebrating the Tsampa festival—an ancient holiday" that does not exist, said one Lhasan, laughing. As soon as Communist Party leaders discovered that Tibetans were celebrating the award under the guise of a nonexistent holiday, they ordered a crackdown. Troops cleared the summer palace and closed it to Tibetans for three days.

Authorities launched a search for the organizers of the "secessionist activities," as they labeled the celebration, according to several sources, including a Tibet government official. More than 200 Tibetans were detained and interrogated.

The arrests in Lhasa and attacks on the Dalai Lama infuriated Tibetans, triggering a wave of demonstrations calling for an end to Chinese rule in Tibet, said Chinese and Tibetan sources. The demonstrations began in October and despite continuing arrests, have persisted, residents said.

On Dec. 5, a group of monks gathered at the center of Barkhor Square, where the Jokhang temple is located, the traditional stage of anti-Chinese demonstrations in Lhasa, and shouted, "Long live the Dalai Lama! Tibet for Tibetans!" They were dragged away by armed police, Tibetan witnesses said. Troops armed with machine guns took up positions in all buildings surrounding the square, including the temple, and public announcements over loud-speakers warned that troops had been ordered to shoot on sight anyone who joined the "separatist" demonstration, residents said.

Despite the warning, Nobel Peace Prize celebrations and anti-Chinese protests were held in the Tibetan quarter of Lhasa, outside of Barkhor Square, on Dec. 7, 9 and 10, according to Tibetan and foreign sources. "Lhasa is counting down toward an explosion right now," said one Tibetan.

In mid-October six monks chanting "Tibetans want independence" marched to Barkhor Square and shouted demands for an end to Chinese killings of Tibetans and the withdrawal of troops from the region, according to several witnesses. Within minutes, they were taken away by troops. One demonstrator's arms were broken for refusing to identify other pro-independence activists, said sources with police contacts.

At a mass rally held by the Lhasa Public Security Bureau a week later, four of the monks were sentenced to three years of labor reform, without trial, for "attempting to split the motherland," a charge that amounts to treason under Chinese law, according to the Nov. 6 edition of the *Tibet Daily*.

In an effort to eradicate Tibetan nationalism, regional party authorities sent teams into Lhasa's major monasteries to conduct "reeducation" sessions, monks and Chinese officials said.

"Most monks in Lhasa must attend these thought reform classes on a regular basis," said one monk. "Sometimes during the meeting, security officials search the monastery and our living quarters for pro-independence literature and newspapers or tapes containing information about the Dalai Lama."

Tibet: A Historical Perspective
by Michael C. van Walt van Praag

The Tibetan Government-in-exile, headed by His Holiness the Dalai Lama, Tibet's exiled head of state and spiritual leader, has consistently held that Tibet has been under illegal Chinese occupation since China invaded the independent state in 1949/50. The People's Republic of China (PRC) insists that its relation with Tibet is purely an internal affair, because Tibet is and has been for centuries an integral part of China. The question of Tibet's status is essentially a legal question, albeit one of immediate political relevance.

The PRC makes no claim to sovereign rights over Tibet as a result of its military subjugation and occupation of Tibet following its armed invasion in 1949/50. Indeed, the PRC could hardly make that claim, since it categorically rejects as illegal claims to sovereignty put forward by other states based on conquest, occupation, or the inposition of unequal treaties. Instead, the PRC bases its claim to Tibet solely on the theory that Tibet became an integral part of China seven hundred years ago.

EARLY HISTORY
Although the history of the Tibetan state started in 127 B.C., with the establishment of the Yarlung Dynasty, the country as

we know it was first unified in the seventh century A.D., under King Songtsen Gampo and his successors. Tibet was one of the mightiest powers of Asia for the three centuries that followed, as a pillar inscription at the foot of the Potala Palace in Lhasa and Chinese Tang histories of the period confirm. A formal peace treaty concluded between China and Tibet in 821/823 demarcated the borders between the two countries and ensured that "Tibetans shall be happy in Tibet and Chinese shall be happy in China."

MONGOL INFLUENCE

As Genghis Khan's Mongol Empire expanded towards Europe in the west and China in the east in the thirteenth century, Tibetan leaders of the powerful Sakya school of Tibetan Buddhism concluded an agreement with the Mongol rulers in order to avoid the conquest of Tibet. The Tibetan Lama promised political loyalty and religious blessings and teachings in exchange for patronage and protection. The religious relationship became so important that when, decades later, Kublai Khan conquered China and established the Yuan Dyansty (1279-1368), he invited the Sakya Lama to become the Imperial Preceptor and supreme pontiff of his empire.

The relationship that developed and continued to exist into the twentieth century between the Mongols and Tibetans was a reflection of the close racial, cultural, and especially religious affinity between the two Central Asian peoples. The Mongol Empire was a world empire and, whatever the relationship between its rulers and the Tibetans, the Mongols never integrated the administration of Tibet and China or appended Tibet to China in any manner.

Tibet broke political ties with the Yuan emperor in 1350, before China regained its independence from the Mongols. Not until the eighteenth century did Tibet again come under a degree of foreign influence.

RELATIONS WITH MANCHU, GORKHA AND BRITISH NEIGHBORS

Tibet developed no ties with the Chinese Ming Dynasty (1386-1644). On the other hand, the Dalai Lama, who established his sovereign rule over Tibet with the help of a Mongol patron in 1642, did develop close religious ties with the Manchu emperors, who conquered China and established the Qing Dynasty (1644-1911). The Dalai Lama agreed to become the spiritual guide of the Manchu emperor, and accepted patronage and protection in exchange. This "priest-patron" relationship (known in Tibetan as Choe-Yoen), which the Dalai Lama also maintained with some Mongol princes and Tibetan nobles, was the only formal tie that existed between the Tibetans and Manchus during the Qing Dynasty. It did not, in itself, affect Tibet's independence.

On the political level, some powerful Manchu emperors succeeded in exerting a degree of influence over Tibet. Thus, between 1720 and 1792, Emperors Kangxi, Yong Zhen, and Qianlong sent imperial troops to Tibet four times to protect the Dalai Lama and the Tibetan people from foreign invasions by Mongols and Gorkhas or from internal unrest. These expeditions provided the Emperor with the means for establishing influence in Tibet. He sent representatives to the Tibetan capital, Lhasa, some of whom successfully exercised their influence in his name over the Tibetan Government, particularly with respect to the conduct of foreign relations. At the height of Manchu power, which lasted a few decades, the situation was not unlike that which can exist between a superpower and a satellite or protectorate, and therefore one which, though politically significant, does not extinguish the independent existence of the weaker state. Tibet was never incorporated into the Manchu Empire, much less China, and it continued to conduct its relations with neighboring states largely on its own.

Manchu influence did not last very long. It was entirely ineffective by the time the British briefly invaded Lhasa and concluded a bilateral treaty with Tibet, the Lhasa Convention, in 1904. Despite this loss of influence, the imperial government in Peking continued to claim some authority over Tibet, particularly with respect to its international relations, an authority which the British imperial government termed "suzerainty" in its dealings with Peking and St. Petersburg, Russia. Chinese imperial armies tried to reassert actual influence in 1910 by invading the country and occupying Lhasa. Following the 1911 revolution in China and the overthrow of the Manchu Empire, the troops surrendered to a Tibetan army and were repatriated under a Sino-Tibetan peace accord. The Dalai Lama reasserted Tibet's full independence internally, by issuing a proclamation, and externally, in communications to foreign rulers and in a treaty with Mongolia.

TIBET IN THE TWENTIETH CENTURY

Tibet's status following the expulsion of Manchu troops is not subject to serious dispute. Whatever ties existed between the Dalai Lamas and the Manchu emperors of the Qing Dynasty were extinguished with the fall of that empire and dynasty. From 1911 to 1950, Tibet successfully avoided undue foreign influence and behaved in every respect as a fully independent state.

Tibet maintained diplomatic relations with Nepal, Bhutan, Britain, and later with independent India. Relations with China remained strained. The Chinese waged a border war with Tibet while formally urging Tibet to "join" the Chinese Republic, claiming all along to the world that Tibet already was one of China's "five races."

In an effort to reduce Sino-Tibetan tensions, the British convened a tripartite conference in Simla in 1913 where the representatives of the three states met on equal terms. As the British delegate reminded his Chinese counterpart, Tibet entered the conference as an "independent nation recognizing no allegiance to China." The conference was unsuccessful in that it did not resolve the differences between Tibet and China. It was, nevertheless, significant in that Anglo-Tibetan friendship was reaffirmed with the conclusion of bilateral trade and border agreements. In a Joint Declaration, Great Britain and Tibet bound themselves not to recognize Chinese suzerainty or other special rights in Tibet unless China signed the draft Simla Convention which would have guaranteed Tibet's greater borders, its territorial integrity and full autonomy. China never signed the Convention, however, leaving the terms of the Joint Declaration in full force.

Tibet conducted its international relations primarily by dealing with the British, Chinese, Nepalese, and Bhutanese diplomatic missions in Lhasa, but also through government delegations traveling abroad. When India became independent, the British mission in Lhasa was replaced by an Indian one. During World War II Tibet remained neutral, despite combined pressure from the United States, Great Britain, and China to allow passage of raw materials through Tibet.

Tibet never maintained extensive international relations, but those countries with whom it did maintain relations treated Tibet as they would any sovereign state. Its international status was in fact no different from, say, that of Nepal. Thus, when Nepal applied for membership in the United Nations in 1949, it cited its treaty and diplomatic relations with Tibet to demonstrate its full international personality.

THE INVASION OF TIBET

The turning point in Tibet's history came in 1949, when the People's Liberation Army of the PRC first crossed into Tibet. After defeating the small Tibetan army and occupying half the country, the Chinese government imposed the so-called "17-Point Agreement for the Peaceful Liberation of Tibet" on the Tibetan government in May 1951. Because it was signed under duress, the agreement lacked validity under international law. The presence of forty thousand troops in Tibet, the threat of an immediate occupation of Lhasa, and the prospect of the total obliteration of the Tibetan state left the Tibetans little choice.

As open resistance to the Chinese occupation escalated, particularly in Eastern Tibet, the Chinese repression, which included the destruction of religious buildings and the imprisonment of monks and other community leaders, increased dramatically. By 1959, popular uprisings culminated in massive demonstrations in Lhasa. By the time China crushed the uprising, 87,000 Tibetans were dead in the Lhasa region alone, and the Dalai Lama had fled to India, where he now heads the Tibetan Government-in-exile, headquartered in Dharamsala, India.

In 1963 the Dalai Lama promulgated a constitution for a democratic Tibet. It has been successfully implemented, to the extent possible, by the Government-in-exile.

Meanwhile, in Tibet religious persecution, consistent violations of human rights, and the wholesale destruction of religious and historic buildings by the occupying authorities have not succeeded in destroying the spirit of the Tibetan people to resist the destruction of their national identity. 1.2 million Tibetans have lost their lives (over one-sixth of the population) as a result of the Chinese occupation. But the new generation of Tibetans seems just as determined to regain the country's independence as the older generation was.

CONCLUSION

In the course of Tibet's two-thousand-year history, the country came under a degree of foreign influence only for short periods of time in the thirteenth and eighteenth centuries. Few independent countries today can claim as impressive a record. As the ambassador of Ireland at the U.N. remarked during the General Assembly debates on the question of Tibet, "for thousands of years, or for a couple of thousand years at any rate, [Tibet] was as free and as fully in control of its own affairs as any nation in this Assembly, and a thousand times more free to look after its own affairs than many of the nations here."

Numerous other countries made statements in the course of the U.N. debates that reflected similar recognition of Tibet's independent status. Thus, for example, the delegate from the Philippines declared, "It is clear that on the eve of the invasion in 1950 Tibet was not under the rule of any foreign country." The delegate from Thailand reminded the assembly that the majority of states "refute the contention that Tibet is part of China." The United States joined most other U.N. members in condemning Chinese aggression and invasion of Tibet. In 1959, 1960, and 1961, the U.N. General Assembly passed resolutions (1353 (XIV), 1723 (XVI), and 2079 (XX)) condemning Chinese human rights abuses in Tibet and calling on that country to respect the fundamental freedoms of the Tibetan people, including their right to self-determination.

From a legal standpoint, Tibet has not lost its statehood. It is an independent state under illegal occupation. Neither China's military invasion nor the continuing occupation by the PLA has transferred the sovereignty of Tibet to China. As pointed out earlier, the Chinese government has never claimed to have acquired sovereignty over Tibet by conquest. Indeed, China recognizes that the use or threat of force (outside the exceptional circumstances provided for in the U.N. Charter), the imposition of an unequal treaty, or the continued illegal occupation of a country can never grant an invader legal title to territory. Its claims are based solely on the alleged subjection of Tibet to a few of China's strongest foreign rulers in the thirteenth and eighteenth centuries.

How can China, one of the most ardent opponents of imperialism and colonialism, defend its continued presence in Tibet against the wishes of the Tibetan people by citing Mongol and Manchu imperialism and its own colonial policies as justification?

72

FURTHER READING

Selected Books by and about the Dalai Lama

The Dalai Lama: A Policy of Kindness (Ithaca: Snow Lion, 1990)
The Bodhgaya Interviews (Ithaca: Snow Lion, 1988)
The Dalai Lama at Harvard (Ithaca: Snow Lion, 1988)
Kindness, Clarity, and Insight (Ithaca: Snow Lion, 1984)
My Land and My People (New York: Potala, 1983)
A Long Look Homeward: An Interview with the Dalai Lama of Tibet, by Glenn H. Mullin (Ithaca: Snow Lion, 1987)
Freedom in Exile (New York: Harper & Row, forthcoming 1990)

General Works on the History of Tibet

Avedon, John F. *In Exile from the Land of Snows* (New York: Vintage, 1986).

Avedon, John F. *Tibet Today: Current Conditions and Prospects* (London: Wisdom Publications, 1988).

Shakabpa, Tsepon W.D. *Tibet: A Political History* (New York: Potala Publications, 1984).

van Walt van Praag, Michael C. *The Status of Tibet* (Boulder: Westview Press, 1987).

These and many other titles on Tibet and Tibetan culture may be obtained from Snow Lion Publications.

Snow Lion Publications
P.O. Box 6483
Ithaca, NY 14851

Write for a catalog or call toll free 1-800-950-0313 or 1-607-273-8519.

Snow Lion Publications is dedicated to the preservation of Tibetan culture.

Current information on Tibet is published in *Tibet Press Watch*, a monthly compilation of materials from international sources and also *News Tibet* which is published three times per year.

Tibet Press Watch
International Campaign for Tibet
Attn: Sonam Tsepal
1511 K Street, NW, Suite 739
Washington, D.C. 20005

News Tibet
The Office of Tibet
107 E. 31 Street, 4th Fl.
New York, NY 10016